START TO SEW

All the Basics PLUS Learn-to-Sew Projects

WITHDRAWN

CREATIVE
PUBLISHING
international

CHANHASSEN, MINNESOTA

Copyright © 2005
Creative Publishing international, Inc.
18705 Lake Drive East
Chanhassen, Minnesota 55317
1-800-328-3895
www.creativepub.com
All rights reserved

President/CEO: Ken Fund
Vice President/Publisher: Linda Ball
Vice President/Retail Sales: Kevin Haas
Executive Editor/Lifestyles: Alison Brown Cerier

START TO SEW

Created by: The Editors of Creative Publishing
international, Inc.

Start to sew : all the basics plus learn-to-sew projects / by the editors of Creative
Publishing International, Inc.
    p. cm.
  ISBN 1-58923-206-2 (soft cover)
  1. Sewing.
  TT710.S73 2004
  646.2--dc22

                            2004021338

Printed in China:
  10 9 8 7 6 5 4 3 2 1

The content of this book has been excerpted from
Sewing 101 and *Home Décor Sewing 101*, published
by Creative Publishing international, Inc.

CONTENTS

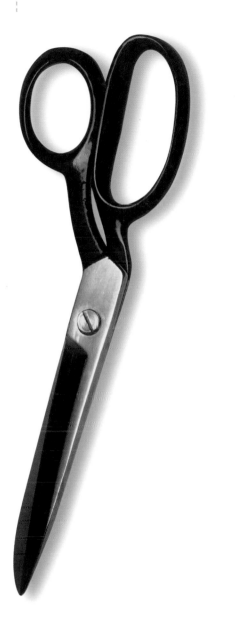

HOW TO USE THIS BOOK

Refer to the **Quick References** at the right side of the pages for definitions or elaborations on any words or phrases printed *like this* on the page. If the word or phrase is followed by a page number, its reference can be found on the page indicated. Words printed **LIKE THIS** can be found in the **Glossary** on pages 63 and 64.

Sewing TOOLS

Sewing tools and supplies help you complete your projects successfully. Here are some measuring, marking, and cutting tools that make sewing easier.

MEASURING AND MARKING TOOLS

A Transparent ruler allows you to see what you are measuring and marking. It also is used to check fabric **GRAINLINES**.

B Yardstick (meterstick) should be made of smooth hardwood or metal.

C Tape measure has the flexibility helpful for measuring items with shape and dimension. Select one made of a material that will not stretch.

D Seam gauge is a 6" (15 cm) metal or plastic ruler with a sliding marker. It helps make quick, accurate measurements and can be used to measure seam allowance widths.

E Transparent T-square is used to locate grainlines and to measure 90° angles.

F Marking chalk is available in several forms: as powder in a rolling wheel dispenser, as a pencil, or as a flat slice. Chalk lines are easily removable from most fabrics.

G Fabric marking pens are available in both air-erasable and water-erasable forms. Air-erasable marks disappear in 48 hours; water-erasable marks wash off with a sprinkling of water.

H Narrow masking tape is an alternative method for marking fabrics when other methods are less suitable.

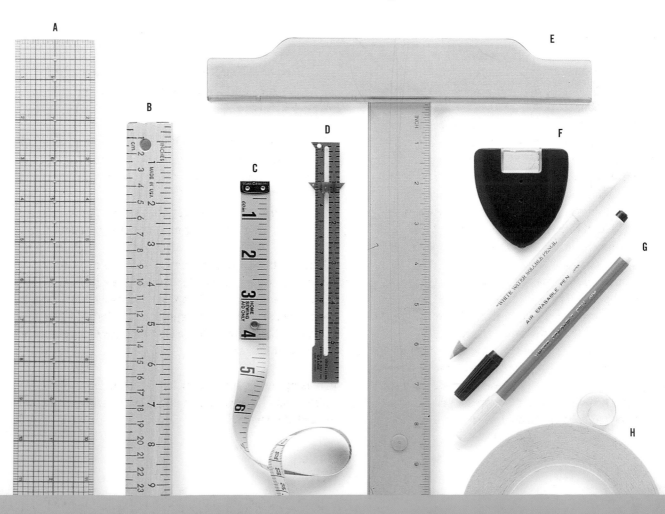

CUTTING TOOLS

Buy quality cutting tools and use them only for your sewing! Cutting paper or other household materials will dull your cutting tools quickly. Dull tools are not only tiresome to work with, they can also damage fabric. Scissors have both handles the same size; shears have one handle larger than the other. The best-quality scissors and shears are hot-forged, high-grade steel, honed to a fine cutting edge. Blades should be joined with an adjustable screw to ensure even pressure along the length of the blade. Have your cutting tools sharpened periodically by a qualified professional.

I Bent-handled dressmaker's shears are best for cutting fabric shapes because the angle of the lower blade lets fabric lie flat on the cutting surface. Blade lengths of 7" or 8" (18 or 20.5 cm) are most popular, but lengths of up to 12" (30.5 cm) are available. Select a blade length appropriate for the size of your hand; shorter lengths for smaller hands. Left-handed models are also available. If you intend to sew a great deal, invest in a pair of all-steel, chrome-plated shears for heavy-duty

cutting. Lighter models with stainless steel blades and plastic handles are fine for less-frequent sewing or lightweight fabrics.

J Sewing scissors have one pointed and one rounded tip for clipping threads and trimming and clipping seam allowances. A 6" (15 cm) blade is suitable for most tasks.

K Seam ripper quickly removes stitches and opens buttonholes. Use it carefully to avoid cutting the fabric.

L Rotary cutter works like a pizza cutter and can be used by left-handed or right-handed sewers. A locking mechanism retracts the blade for safety. Use the rotary cutter with a special plastic mat available in different sizes, with or without grid lines. The self-healing mat protects both the work surface and the blade.

M Pinking shears and pinking rotary cutters are used to finish seams. They cut fabric in a zigzag or scalloped pattern instead of a straight line.

Special PRODUCTS

Many special products and gadgets are designed to assist you in various steps of the sewing process. Before using a new product, read the manufacturer's instructions carefully. Learn what special handling or care is required, and for what fabrics or sewing techniques the product is suited. Here are some specialized products, available in fabric stores, that you may find helpful in sewing your clothes, accessories, or home décor items.

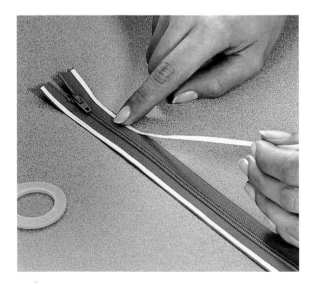

Basting tape is double-faced adhesive tape used instead of pinning or basting. It is especially helpful for matching prints, applying zippers, and positioning trims. Some manufacturers advise that you avoid stitching through the tape because the adhesive may collect on your needle.

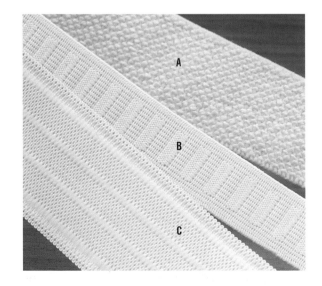

Elastics can be purchased in a variety of widths and styles, either in precut packages or by the yard (meter). Softer elastics **(A)** are suitable for pajamas or boxer shorts; nonroll elastic **(B)** stays flat in the casing; some wide elastic has channels for topstitching **(C)**.

Dodkin is used to thread elastic or cording through a **CASING**. One end holds the elastic or cord tightly while you feed the tool through the narrow casing.

Welting is a fabric-covered cording, sewn into a seam or around an outer edge to provide extra strength and a decorative finishing touch. It is available in many colors and various diameters to purchase by the yard (meter) or in precut packaged lengths.

Point turner is helpful for perfecting corners, such as at the top of a pocket, at the ends of a waistband, or inside a pillow cover. Slip the tool inside the item, and gently poke the fabric out into a point.

Interfacing plays a supporting role in almost every garment. It is an inner layer of fabric, used to stabilize the fabric in areas like necklines and waistbands, or give support behind buttons and buttonholes. Interfacings may be woven, nonwoven, or knit; the easiest forms to use are heat fusible.

Fabric INFORMATION

Selecting the right fabrics for your projects may seem like an overwhelming task, but there are a few simple guidelines to help narrow the field.

WOVEN FABRICS

Woven fabrics have straight lengthwise and crosswise yarns. The pattern in which the yarns are woven gives the fabric its characteristic surface texture and appearance. The outer edges of woven fabrics are called **SELVAGES**. As a general rule, they should be trimmed away because they are often heavier than the rest of the fabric, and they may shrink when laundered or pressed. **GRAINLINES** are the directions in which the fabric yarns run. Strong, stable lengthwise yarns, running parallel to the selvages, form the **LENGTHWISE GRAIN**. The **CROSSWISE GRAIN** is perpendicular to the lengthwise grain and has a small amount of give. Any diagonal direction, called the **BIAS**, has a fair amount of stretch.

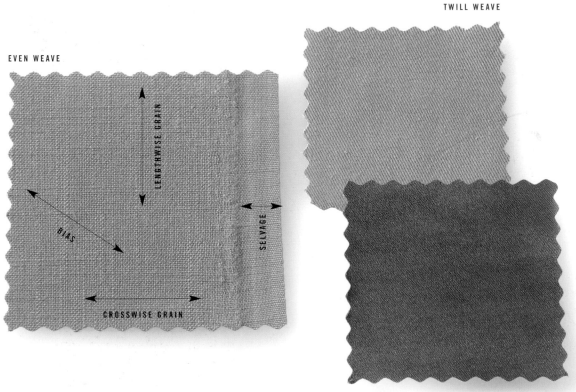

TWILL WEAVE

EVEN WEAVE

LENGTHWISE GRAIN

BIAS

SELVAGE

CROSSWISE GRAIN

SATIN WEAVE

KNIT FABRICS

Knit fabrics consist of rows of interlocking loops of yarn, as in a hand-knit sweater, but usually on a finer scale. Knit fabrics are more flexible than other fabrics, and they all stretch. These features mean that garments made of knits require less fitting and offer more freedom of movement. When sewing with knits, select patterns that are specifically designed for knit fabrics.

Knit fabric is made from interlocking looped stitches. The lengthwise rows of stitches are called **RIBS**; the crosswise rows are called **COURSES**. These ribs and courses correspond to the lengthwise and crosswise grains of woven fabrics.

Patterns designed for knit fabrics have a stretch gauge. Fold over the fabric along a crosswise course several inches (centimeters) from a cut end, and test its degree of stretch against the gauge. If the fabric stretches the necessary amount without distortion, it is suitable for the pattern.

STRETCH TERRY

SYNTHETIC FLEECE

DOUBLE KNIT

SWEATSHIRT FLEECE

NOVELTY KNIT

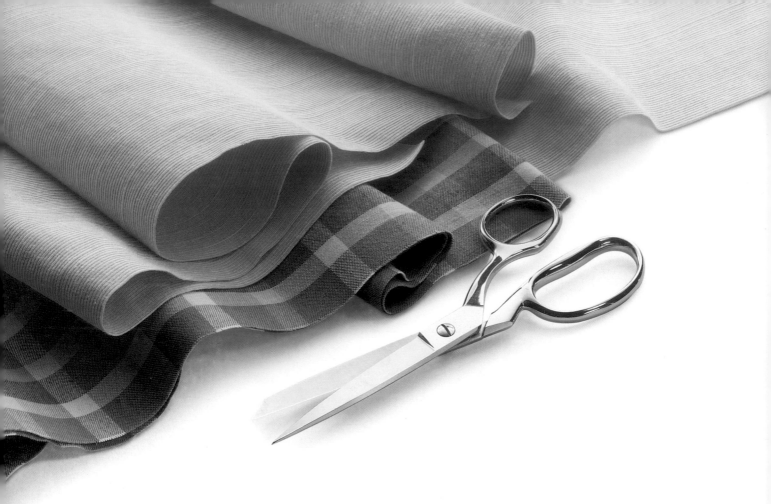

Cutting DECORATOR FABRICS

Cutting into a new piece of fabric may seem a little scary, considering the investment you have just made. Here are a few guidelines for accurate cutting that should boost your confidence.

After preshrinking, straighten the cut ends of the fabric, using one of the three methods opposite. Then mark the other cutting lines, using the straightened edge as a guide. Before cutting full-width pieces of fabric for large home décor projects, such as tablecloths, window swags, or Roman shades, pin-mark the placement of each cut along the **SELVAGE**. Mark out pieces for smaller projects, like decorator pillows or napkins, with chalk. Double-check your measurements and inspect the fabric for flaws. Once you have cut into the fabric, you cannot return it. To ensure that large décor items will hang or lay straight, the fabric lengths must be cut on-grain. This means that the cuts are made along the exact **CROSSWISE GRAIN** of the fabric. Patterned decorator fabrics are cut following the **PATTERN REPEAT** rather than the grainline so they must be *printed on-grain*.

For tightly woven fabrics without a matchable pattern, mark straight cuts on the crosswise grain, using a carpenter's square. Align one edge to a selvage and mark along the perpendicular side.

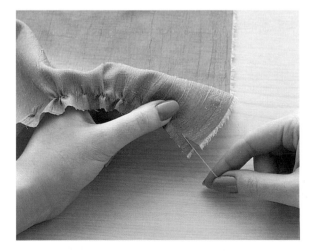

For loosely woven fabrics, such as linen tablecloth fabric, pull out a yarn along the crosswise grain, from selvage to selvage. Cut along the line left by the missing yarn.

QUICK REFERENCE

Printed on-grain. This means the pattern repeat coincides exactly with the crosswise grain of the fabric. To test fabric before you buy, place it on a flat surface and fold the cut edge back, aligning the selvages on the sides. Crease the fold with your fingers, then unfold the fabric and check to see if the crease runs into the selvage at exactly the same point in the pattern on both sides. Slight differences of less than 2" (5 cm) can usually be corrected by stretching the fabric diagonally. Avoid buying fabric that is printed more that 2" (5 cm) off-grain, as you will not be able to correct it, and the finished project will not hang straight.

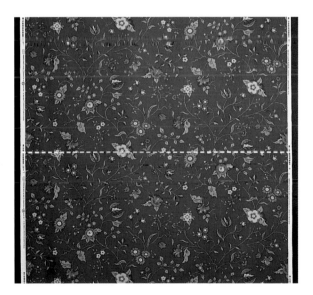

For tightly woven patterned decorator fabric, mark both selvages at the exact same point in the pattern repeat. Using a long straightedge, draw a line connecting the two points. If you will be stitching two or more full widths of fabric together, make all the cuts at the same location in the repeat. This usually means that you cut the pieces longer than necessary, stitch them together, and then trim them to the necessary length.

Pattern LAYOUT

All pattern companies use a universal system of symbols on their pattern pieces. These symbols help you lay out the pattern, show you where to cut, help you match up seamlines, show you where to sew, and give placement guides for things like buttons, buttonholes, and hems. Along with the symbols, essential instructions are printed on the pattern pieces.

Foldline. Often indicated by a long bracket with arrows at each end, it may have "place on fold" instructions. Place the pattern piece with the foldline exactly on the fold of the fabric.

Dots (large and small), squares, or triangles found along the seamlines indicate areas of construction where precise matching, clipping, or stitching is essential.

Grainline. Heavy solid line with arrows at each end. Place the pattern piece on the fabric with the grainline running parallel to the SELVAGE.

Adjustment line. Double line indicating where the pattern can be lengthened or shortened before cutting out the fabric. If an alteration is necessary, cut the pattern on the double line; spread evenly to lengthen, or overlap evenly to shorten.

Seamlines. Long, broken line, usually 5/8" (1.5 cm) inside the cutting line. Multisize patterns often do not have seamlines printed on them.

Cutting line. Heavy solid line along the outer edge of the pattern, often shown with a scissors symbol. Cut on this line. When more than one size is printed on one pattern, the cutting lines may be various styles of solid, dotted, or dashed lines, to help you distinguish one size from the next.

Notches. Diamond shapes along the cutting line, used for matching seams. They may be numbered in the order in which the seams are joined.

Button and buttonhole placement marks. Solid lines indicate the length of the buttonhole, if you are using the button size suggested on the pattern back. "X" or a button symbol shows the button size and placement.

Detail positions. Broken or solid lines indicating the placement for pockets or other details. Mark the position for accurate placement.

Hemline. Hem allowance is printed on the cutting line. Turn the hem up the specified amount, adjusting as necessary.

CONTINUED

Pattern LAYOUT

CONTINUED

Prepare a large work area, such as a dining room table covered with a cutting board. Assemble all the pattern pieces you will be needing, and press out any wrinkles with a warm, dry iron.

Locate and circle the correct pattern layout diagram on your pattern guide sheet, as shown opposite. These diagrams usually show you the easiest, most efficient way to lay out your pattern. Some fabrics have a **NAP**, meaning they have definite up and down directions. For these fabrics, pattern pieces must all be laid out in the same direction.

Fold the fabric in half, lengthwise. Smooth it out on the work surface, so that the **SELVAGES** align and the **CROSSWISE GRAIN** is perpendicular to them. Arrange the pattern pieces as indicated in the layout diagram. White pattern shapes indicate the piece is to be placed with the printed side up. Shaded pieces are to be placed with the printed side down. Be sure to follow any other incidental directions that pertain to your layout. After all the pieces are in place, pin them to the fabric. Do not begin cutting until all the pattern pieces are in place.

PINNING

First, position the pattern pieces that are to be cut on the fold. Place each one directly on the folded edge of the fabric. Pin the corners diagonally. Then continue pinning near the outer edge, placing the pins parallel to the cutting line. Space the pins about 3" (7.5 cm) apart; closer together on curves.

Place the straight-grain pattern pieces on the fabric, with the grainline arrow parallel to the selvages on woven fabrics or parallel to the **RIBS** on knits. Measure from each end of the arrow to the selvage, shifting the pattern until the distances are equal. Pin both ends of the grainline so the pattern will not shift. Then pin the outer edges.

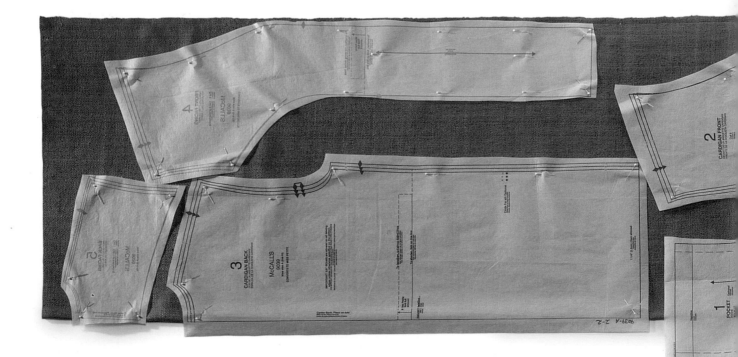

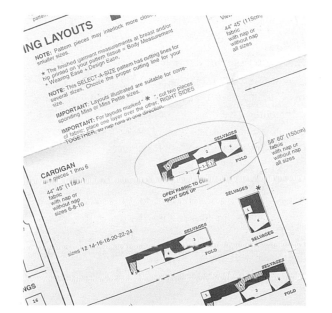

QUICK REFERENCE

Fold the fabric in half, lengthwise. When your fabric is folded like this, you will end up with mirror-image pieces for the left and right sides of the garment. Pattern directions usually suggest folding right sides together. Sometimes there are advantages to folding wrong sides together, such as having a better view of the fabric design or ease in marking. Either way will work.

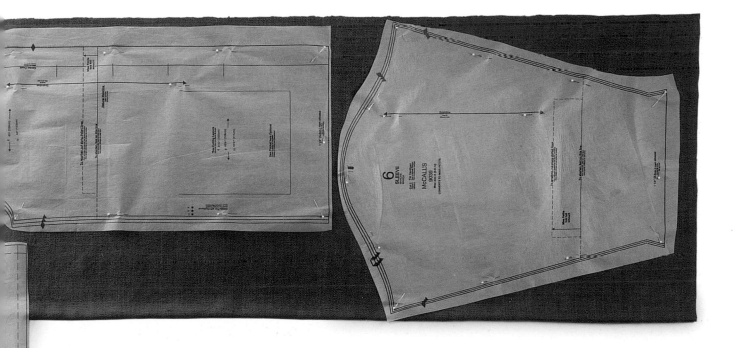

Cutting and MARKING

Don't be intimidated! Locate the correct cutting lines, and cut with confidence. Transfer the necessary marks, and you'll be ready to sew!

CUTTING

Accuracy is important, since mistakes made in cutting cannot always be corrected. Before cutting, double-check the placement of the pattern pieces.

Using bent-handled shears, cut with long, firm strokes, cutting directly on the cutting line. Take shorter strokes around curves. If you are using a multisize pattern, be sure that you follow the correct cutting line all the time.

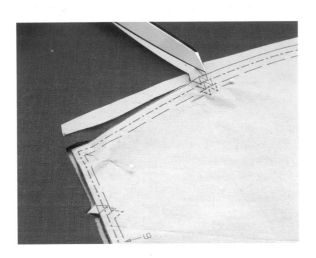

Notches can be cut outward, especially if the fabric is loosely woven or if the pattern calls for ¼" (6 mm) **SEAM ALLOWANCES**. Cut multiple notches as one unit, not separately. Or, you can cut directly through the notches, and then mark them with short snips into the seam allowances.

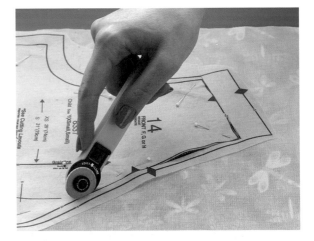

If you prefer to use a **ROTARY CUTTER AND MAT**, be sure to keep the mat under the area being cut. Use steady, even pressure, and, above all, keep fingers and small children away from the rotary cutter.

MARKING

Keep the pattern pieces pinned in place after cutting. Transfer pattern symbols to the appropriate side of the fabric, using one of the following methods.

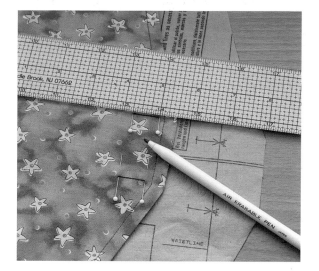

Erasable fabric markers are felt-tip pens designed specifically for sewing needs. Air-erasable marks disappear within 48 hours. Water-erasable marks disappear with a spritz of water.

Pins are a quick way to transfer marks. Since they may fall out easily, use pin marks only when you intend to sew immediately. Or pin-mark first, remove the pattern, and mark again, using chalk or erasable fabric marker.

Snips are handy for marking things like dots at shoulder seams. Make shallow snips into the seam allowances at the dot locations.

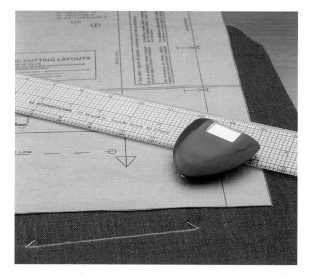

Chalk is available in pencil form or as a powder in a rolling-wheel dispenser.

Sewing a **SEAM**

Little frustrations, such as thread jams, erratic stitching lines, or having the thread pull out of the needle at the start of a seam, can often be prevented or corrected by following these basic guidelines. If you are really not sure where to begin, then you should probably begin right here!

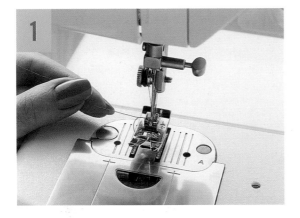

1 Thread your machine and insert the bobbin. Holding the needle thread with your left hand, turn the handwheel toward you until the needle has gone down and come back up to its highest point. A stitch will form, and you will feel a tug on the needle thread. Pull on the needle thread to bring the bobbin thread up through the hole in the throat plate. Pull both threads together under the presser foot and off to one side.

2 Cut two pieces of fabric and place them right sides together, aligning the outer edges. Pin the pieces together along one long edge, *inserting the pins* about every 2" (5 cm), *perpendicular to the edge.* Place the fabric under the presser foot so the pinned side edges align to the 1/2" (1.3 cm) *seam allowance guide* and the upper edges are just behind the opening of the presser foot. Lower the presser foot, and set your stitch length at 2.5 mm, which equals 10 stitches per inch.

3 Begin by *backstitching* several stitches to the upper edge of the fabric. Hold the thread tails under a finger for the first few stitches. This prevents the needle thread from being pulled out of the needle and also prevents the thread tails from being drawn down into the bobbin case, where they could potentially cause the dreaded **THREAD JAM.**

4 Stitch forward over the backstitched line, and continue sewing the 1/2" (1.3 cm) seam. Gently guide the fabric while you sew by walking your fingers ahead of and slightly to the sides of the presser foot. Remember, you are only guiding; let the machine pull the fabric.

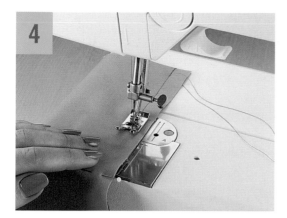

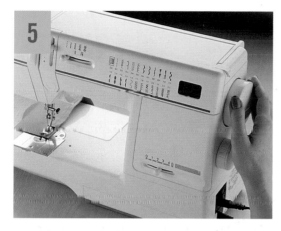

5 Stop stitching and *remove pins as you come to them*. When you reach the end of the fabric, stop stitching; backstitch several stitches, and stop again. Turn the handwheel toward you until the needle is in its highest position.

6 Raise the presser foot. *Remove the fabric from the machine*.

QUICK REFERENCE

Inserting the pins perpendicular to the edge. In this position, the pin heads are near the raw edge where you can easily grasp them with your right hand. You are also much less likely to stick yourself with a pin as you sew.

Seam allowance guide. Most machines have a series of lines on the throat plate. These lines mark the distance from the needle (where a standard straight stitch seam would be) to the cut edges. Measure these lines on your machine to determine where the edge of your fabric should be for the width seam you are stitching.

Backstitching keeps the beginning and end of your stitching line from pulling out. Check your owner's manual to see how to backstitch with your machine. You may need to lift and hold your stitch length lever, push in and hold a button, or simply touch an icon.

Remove pins as you come to them. As tempting as it may be, don't sew over pins! You may be lucky and save a few seconds, or you could hit a pin and break the needle.

Remove the fabric from the machine. Pull the fabric smoothly away from the presser foot, either to the left side or straight back. If you have to tug the threads, turn your handwheel slightly toward you until they pull easily. Cut the threads, leaving tails 2½" to 3" (6.5 to 7.5 cm) long.

TIP Straight stitching lines are easier to achieve if you watch the edge of the fabric along the seam guide and ignore the needle. Sew smoothly at a relaxing pace, with minimal starting and stopping, and without bursts of speed. You have better control of the speed if you operate your foot control with your heel resting on the floor.

STRETCH SEAMS

Aside from the standard straight-stitch **SEAM**, your machine is probably capable of sewing several other stitches that are appropriate for various fabrics and situations. Whenever you sew with knits, for example, you want a seam that will stretch with the fabric.

 TIP The cut edges of knit fabrics do not ravel, but they often curl. To minimize this problem, the seam allowances are usually finished together and pressed to one side.

Double-stitched seam. Stitch on the seamline, using a straight stitch set at a length of 12 stitches per inch, which equals 2 mm long. Stretch the fabric slightly as you sew to allow the finished seam to stretch that much. Stitch again ⅛" (3 mm) into the seam allowance. Trim the seam allowance close to the second stitching line. This seam is appropriate for fabrics with minimal stretch or for seams sewn in the vertical direction on moderate stretch knits.

Narrow zigzag seam. Stitch on the seamline, using a very narrow zigzag stitch set at 12 stitches per inch, which equals 2 mm long. If the fabric is very stretchy in the direction you are sewing, you may also stretch the fabric slightly as you sew. Trim the seam allowance to ¼" (6 mm), if necessary. Set the zigzag wider, and stitch the seam allowance edges together. This seam is appropriate for very stretchy knits.

Built-in stretch stitch. Differing from brand to brand, these stitches are designed to incorporate stretch, so that you do not need to stretch the fabric as you sew. Some stitch styles, like the bottom two samples, are a pattern of zigzag and straight stitches that stitch and finish the seam in one pass. Check your manual for stitch settings.

SEAM FINISHES

To prevent raveling of woven fabrics, **SEAM ALLOWANCE** edges must be finished. There are several finishing methods to choose from, depending on the fabric and the capabilities of your machine.

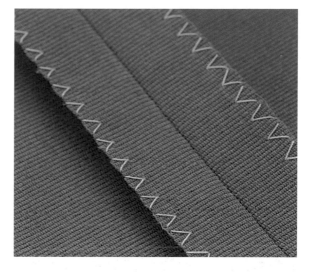

Stitched and pinked finish. Stitch ¼" (6 mm) from each seam allowance edge, using a straight stitch set at 12 stitches per inch, or 2 mm. Trim close to the stitching, using pinking shears (page 5). This finish is suitable for finely woven fabrics that do not ravel easily.

Zigzag finish. Set the zigzag stitch on or near maximum width and a length of 10 stitches per inch, which equals 2.5 mm. Stitch close to the edge of each seam allowance so that the right-hand stitches go just over the edge. If the fabric puckers, try a narrower zigzag width.

Multistitch-zigzag finish. If your machine has this stitch, check your owner's manual for directions on selecting the settings. Stitch near, but not over, the edge of each seam allowance.

Turn and zigzag finish. Set the zigzag stitch near maximum width at a length of 10 stitches per inch, which equals 2.5 mm. Turn under the seam allowance edge ⅛" to ¼" (3 to 6 mm). Stitch close to the folded edge so that the right-hand stitches go just on or over the fold. Use this finish on loosely woven fabrics, especially on garments such as jackets, where the inside may be visible occasionally.

HEMS

There are a number of ways to hem the lower edges of skirts, pants, jackets, and shirts. Some hems are sewn by machine, others by hand. The method you choose will depend on the fabric, the garment style, and your own preference. For methods that do not involve turning under the raw edge, finish the edge (page 21) in an appropriate manner before hemming.

HAND HEMS

Blindstitch. Fold back the finished edge of the hem ¼" (6 mm). Take a small stitch to anchor the thread in a seam allowance. Work with the needle pointing in the direction you are going. Take a small horizontal stitch in the garment, catching only one or two threads. Take the next stitch in the hem, ¼" to ½" (6 mm to 1.3 cm) away from the first stitch. Continue alternating stitches; do not pull too tightly.

Blind catchstitch. Fold back the finished edge of the hem ¼" (6 mm). Take a small stitch to anchor the thread in a seam allowance. Work with the needle pointing in the direction opposite from the way you are going. Take a very small horizontal stitch in the garment, catching only one or two threads. Take the next stitch in the hem, ¼" to ½" (6 mm to 1.3 cm) away from the first stitch, crossing the stitches. Continue alternating the stitches in a zigzag pattern.

Slipstitch. Fold under the raw edge ¼" (6 mm), and press. Take a small stitch to anchor the thread in a seam allowance. Work with the needle pointing in the direction you are going. Follow the directions for slipstitching on page 24, catching only one or two threads with each stitch that goes into the garment.

MACHINE HEMS

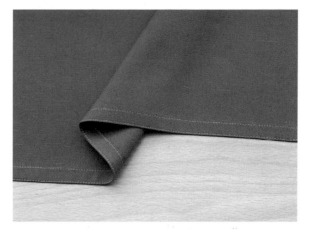

Double-fold hem. This method results in one or two rows of straight stitches showing on the right side of the garment, which is generally a more casual appearance. This method is most successful on straight edges where there is no excess fullness to ease in. See steps 1 to 3 for the napkins on page 45. It may be helpful to hand-baste the folds in place before machine-stitching.

Machine blindstitch. Follow your manual for adjusting the stitch settings, and use the appropriate presser foot. Test the stitch on a scrap of the garment fabric until you are happy with the results. **(A)** Place the hem allowance facedown on the machine bed, with the bulk of the garment folded back. Allow about ¼" (6 mm) of the hem edge to extend under the presser foot, aligning the soft fold to rest against the guide in the foot. Stitch along the hem, close to the fold, catching only one or two threads of the garment with each left-hand stitch of the needle. **(B)** When complete, open out the hem, and press it flat.

Double-needle hem. Stitched from the right side of the fabric, this hem is suitable for knit garments, because it will stretch slightly. The farther apart the needles are spaced, the more stretch the hem will have. However, widely spaced needles will usually produce a ridge between the stitching lines. Using two thread spools on top, thread both needles. Place tape on the bed of the machine as a stitching guide.

Hand STITCHES

While sewers today rely on sewing machines for speedy garment construction, there are situations when hand stitching is necessary or preferable. You may need to slipstitch an opening closed in the lining of a vest, or perhaps you like the look of a hand-stitched blind hem (page 22). Of course, you'll also need to sew on buttons.

THREADING THE NEEDLE

Insert the thread end through the needle's eye, for sewing with a single strand. Or fold the thread in half, and insert the fold through the eye, for sewing with a double strand. Pull through about 8" (20.5 cm). Wrap the other end(s) around your index finger. Then, using your thumb, roll the thread off your finger, twisting it into a knot.

TIP Use a single strand when slipstitching or hemming. Use a double strand when sewing on buttons. To avoid tangles, begin with thread no longer than 18" (46 cm) from the needle to the knot. Run the thread through beeswax, which strengthens the thread and prevents tangling while hand sewing, if desired.

SLIPSTITCHING

1 Insert the threaded needle between the seam allowance and the outer fabric, just behind the opening. Bring it to the outside in the seamline. If you are right-handed, work from right to left; lefties work from left to right.

2 Insert the needle into the fold just behind where the thread came up, and run it inside the fold for about ¼" (6 mm). Bring the needle out, and draw the thread snug. Take your next stitch in the opposite fold, inserting the needle directly across from the previous stitch.

3 Continue, crossing from one fold to the other, until you have sewn past the opening. Secure the thread with several tiny stitches in the seamline. Then take a long stitch, and pull it tight. Clip the thread at the surface, and let the tail disappear inside.

SEWING ON A SHANK BUTTON

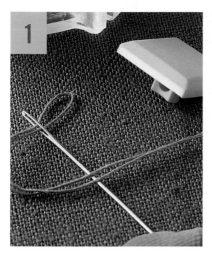

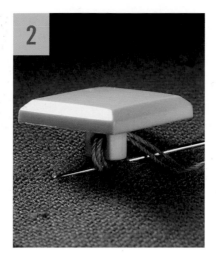

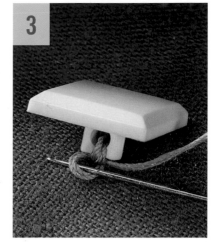

1 Place the button on the mark, with the shank hole parallel to the buttonhole. Secure the thread on the right side of the garment with a small stitch under the button.

2 Bring the needle through the shank hole. Insert the needle down through the fabric and pull the thread through. Take four to six stitches in this manner.

3 Secure the thread in the fabric under the button by making a knot or by taking several small stitches. Clip the thread ends.

SEWING ON A SEW-THROUGH BUTTON

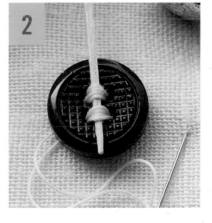

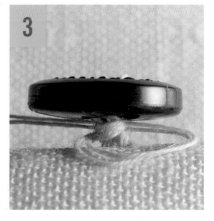

1 Place the button on the mark, with the holes lining up parallel to the buttonhole. Bring the needle through the fabric from the underside and up through one hole in the button. Insert the needle into another hole and through the fabric layers.

2 Slip a toothpick, match, or sewing machine needle between the thread and the button to form a shank. Take three or four stitches through each pair of holes. Bring the needle and thread to the right side under the button. Remove the toothpick.

3 Wind the thread two or three times around the button stitches to form the shank. Secure the thread on the right side under the button, by making a knot or taking several small stitches. Clip the threads close to the knot.

Fleece THROW

When there's a chill in the air, you'll be cuddled up cozy in your fleece throw. Not just for cold-weather climates, synthetic fleece is a comfortable choice for cool southern mornings and evenings, too. The contemporary flowers are raw-edge **APPLIQUÉS** with fleece pompom centers. Because the cut edges of synthetic fleece don't ravel, a throw requires little sewing, and edges can simply be cut into fringe.

WHAT YOU'LL LEARN

How to use a rotary cutter and mat

How to sew raw-edge appliqués

Quick and easy tricks for cutting fringe

Synthetic fleece might be your new favorite fabric

WHAT YOU'LL NEED

2 yd. (1.85 m) polyester fleece for the throw

¼ yd. (0.25 m) fleece for flower appliqués

⅛ yd. (0.15 m) fleece for flower centers

Paper for drawing the appliqué pattern

Rotary cutter and mat

Metal or heavy plastic straightedge

Temporary fabric adhesive

Narrow masking tape; pencil

Thread to match the fabrics

4" (10 cm) square of cardboard

How to Sew a FLEECE THROW

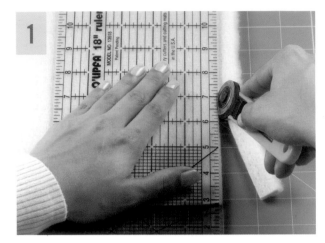

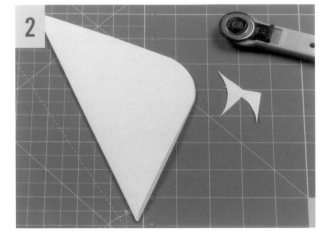

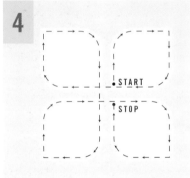

3 Position the flowers in blocks of four petals each, with the square corners at the centers and outer edges of the flowers. Space the petals evenly 3/8" (1 cm) apart. Spray the wrong side of the petals with **TEMPORARY FABRIC ADHESIVE**, following the manufacturer's directions. Adhere them in place.

TIP To protect your work surface from overspray, place the pieces in the bottom of a box.

4 Insert a ballpoint or universal point needle into the machine. Wind a bobbin with thread to match the throw fabric, and insert it into the machine. Thread the upper machine with a color that matches the petals. **EDGESTITCH** around petals of one flower in one continuous stitching line, beginning at the center point of one petal. Stitch slowly around the curves, stopping and turning fabric as needed. **PIVOT** fabric at the square corners. Overlap a few stitches where they meet. Repeat for each of the flowers.

LET'S BEGIN

1 Square off the ends of the fleece and trim off the **SELVAGES**, using a **ROTARY CUTTER AND MAT** (page 5) with a metal or heavy plastic straightedge.

2 Cut out a 5" (12.7 cm) paper square for the appliqué pattern. Fold it in half diagonally, and round the two open corners. Unfold. Using the pattern, cut out 12 flower petals from the appliqué fleece.

TIP By threading the machine in this way, the stitches will be less visible on both sides of the throw. They will simply sink into the fleece. The back of the throw will look as if it has been quilted.

5 Place a strip of narrow masking tape 5" (12.7 cm) from one end of the throw. Mark the tape every 1/2" (1.3 cm). Using a rotary cutter and mat and a straightedge, cut fabric perpendicular to the tape at each mark, fringing the edge. Remove the tape. Repeat at the other end. Tie a knot at the top of each fringe strip, tying all of them in the same direction for best appearance.

TIP You may be able to use the same strip of tape on the opposite end. It only has to be slightly sticky to serve its purpose.

6 Cut the pompom fabric into four 1/2" × 30" (1.3 × 76 cm) strips on the **CROSSWISE GRAIN**; trim off the selvages at the ends. Stretch the strips to make them curl. Cut one of the strips into three pieces for the ties.

7 Wrap a long strip around a 4" (10 cm) square of cardboard. Slide the loops off the cardboard and tie them around the center with a short strip forming a pompom. Cut the loops, if desired. Repeat to make the other pompoms. Trim the tie ends to the same length as the other pieces. Hand-stitch a pompom to the center of each flower.

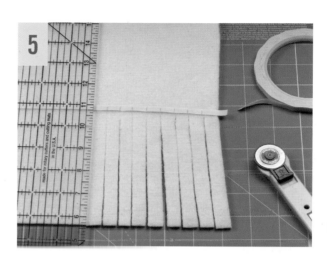

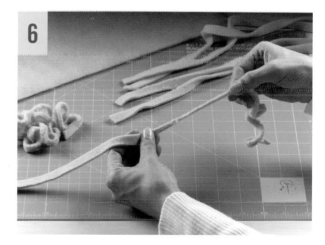

Knife-edge PILLOWS

The knife-edge pillow is probably the most versatile style for decorating your home. There are no limits to the variations you can create, not only in size, color, and texture, but also in added details that give your pillow a personal touch. The directions that follow are for a knife-edge pillow that is 14" (35.5 cm) square. For your first pillow, we recommend a firmly woven mediumweight fabric.

Ready-made knife-edge pillow inserts come in a wide selection of sizes, including 12", 14", 16", 18", 20", 24", and 30" (30.5, 35.5, 40.5, 46, 51, 61, and 76 cm) squares and a 12" × 16" (30.5 × 40.5 cm) rectangle. By adapting these cutting instructions, you can sew a cover for any size pillow insert. You can also use these instructions to sew your own pillow inserts in any size you like, stuffing them to a plumpness that pleases you. Here are instructions for a pillow without or with a zipper.

WHAT YOU'LL LEARN

How to backstitch

How to set and PRESS seams

How to sew perfect corners

How to slipstitch an opening closed by hand

How to insert a zipper

WHAT YOU'LL NEED

14" (35.5 cm) square pillow form

1/2 yd. (0.5 m) fabric

Matching thread

Hand-sewing needle

How to Sew a **KNIFE-EDGE PILLOW**

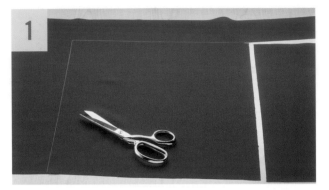

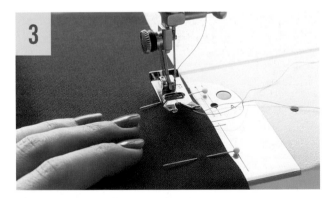

LET'S BEGIN

1 Cut two 15" (38 cm) squares of fabric, aligning the sides to the fabric **GRAINLINES**. A ½" (1.3 cm) **SEAM ALLOWANCE** is needed on each side, so 1" (2.5 cm) is added to each dimension of the desired finished size.

2 Place the pillow front over the pillow back, right sides together, and align all four edges. Pin the layers together near the outer edges, *inserting the pins perpendicular to the edges (p. 19).* In the center of one side, leave a 7" (18 cm) opening unpinned.

3 Place the fabric under the presser foot, just ahead of the opening. Align the cut edges of the fabric to the ½" (1.3 cm) *seam allowance guide (p. 19)* on the bed of your machine. Remove the pin that marks the opening, before lowering the presser foot.

4 *Backstitch (p. 19)* three or four stitches; stop. Then, stitching forward, stitch the seam on all four sides, **PIVOTING** with the needle down at the corners. End the **SEAM** at the opposite side of the opening; backstitch three or four stitches.

5 *Remove the fabric from the machine (p. 19).* Trim the threads close to the fabric. Press the seams flat to set the stitching line in the fabric. This may seem unnecessary, but it really does give you a better-looking seam in the end.

6 Turn back the top seam allowance and press, applying light pressure with the tip of the iron down the crease of the seam. In the area of the opening, turn back and press the top seam allowance 1/2" (1.3 cm). Turn the cover over; turn back and press the remaining opening seam allowance.

7 Turn the pillow cover right side out through the opening. Gently push the points out to form *perfect corners*. Compress and insert the pillow form. Align the pressed edges of the opening, and pin the opening closed. Thread a hand needle and tie a knot in the end.

8 Slipstitch the opening closed, following the instructions on page 24.

QUICK REFERENCE

Perfect corners. The corners of your pillow should be sharply squared, not rounded. To improve the appearance of a slightly rounded corner, you can push a pointed utensil into the corner from inside the pillow cover to force the stitches out to the corner. An inexpensive specialty tool, called a point turner (page 7) works well; or you can use a large knitting needle, a ballpoint pen with the inkball retracted, or something similar. Use light pressure, though, so you don't punch a hole in the corner.

How to Sew a PILLOW WITH A ZIPPER

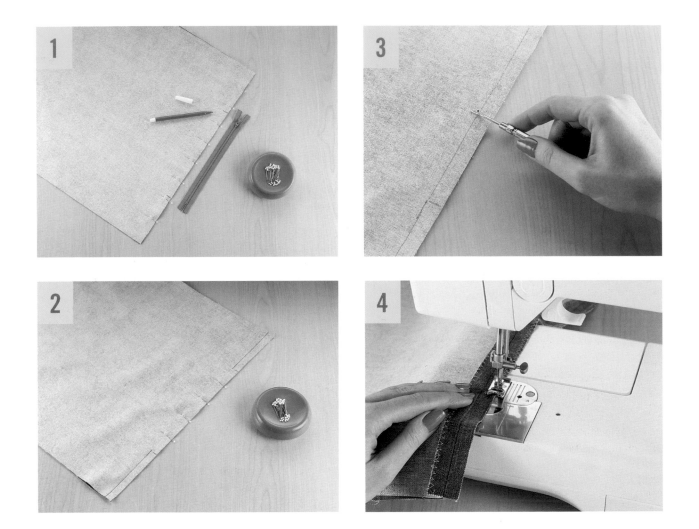

1 Place the pillow front over the pillow back, right sides together. Pin the side that will have the zipper. Center the zipper alongside the pinned edges, and mark the **SEAM ALLOWANCES** just above and below the *zipper stops.*

TIP For best results, select a side that was cut on the **LENGTHWISE GRAIN** of the fabric. The lengthwise grain is more stable and will have less tendency to stretch as you sew.

2 Stitch a ½" (1.3 cm) **SEAM** from the upper edge to the mark, *backstitching (p. 19)* at the beginning and the end. Repeat at the lower edge. Leave the center section open.

3 *Machine-baste* on the seamline between the marks. Clip the basting stitches every 2" (5 cm) with a seam ripper (page 5). This will make the stitches easier to remove later.

4 **PRESS** the seam flat; then press the seam allowances open. *Finish the raw edges* with a **ZIGZAG STITCH.**

TIP If your fabric is loosely woven or tends to ravel easily, repeated washings could make the seam allowances ravel away and ruin your pillow. As a preventative measure, take the time to finish all of the seam allowances.

CONTINUED

QUICK REFERENCE

Zipper stops. Tiny metal bars are attached to the top and bottom of the zipper coil to prevent the zipper slide from sliding right off the end. On a conventional zipper, there is one wide stop at the bottom of the zipper and separate smaller stops at the top.

Machine-baste. Set the stitch length on your machine to sew long stitches. This is done to hold the two fabrics together until they are secured in a seam. Because the stitches are long, the fabric may want to pucker. To avoid this, hold the fabric taut, with one hand in front of the presser foot and the other hand behind it.

Finish the raw edges. Abrasion and laundering will cause yarns to ravel off the raw edges of any woven fabric unless you do something to prevent it. Zigzag stitches sewn over the edge lock the outer yarns in place. This is a suitable way to finish edges that normally don't show.

How to Sew a PILLOW WITH A ZIPPER

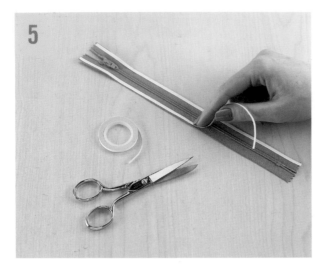

CONTINUED

5 Apply basting tape (page 6) to the right side of the zipper tape, running it along both outer edges.

6 Place the zipper facedown over the seam, with the zipper coil directly over the basted part of the seamline and the pull tab turned down. The zipper coil should be centered between the backstitched areas. Press with your fingers to secure the zipper to the seam allowances.

7 Spread the pillow pieces flat, right side up. Insert pins in the seamline, just above and below the zipper stops. Cut 1/2" (1.3 cm) transparent tape to fit between the pins; place it down the center of the seamline.

8 Attach the zipper foot and adjust it to the left of the needle. If your zipper foot is not adjustable, adjust the needle to the right of the foot. Stitch along the outer edge of the tape, stitching across one end, down one side, and across the other end; **PIVOT** at the corners.

9 Adjust the zipper foot to the right of the needle or adjust your needle to the left of the foot. Stitch over the previous stitches at one end, down the opposite side, and over the stitches at the other end. Clip the threads.

10 Remove the tape. Carefully remove the machine basting in the seamline, using a seam ripper.

11 Open the zipper. Pin the pillow front and back, right sides together, along the three remaining sides. Stitch 1/2" (1.3 cm) seam; press. Turn the pillow cover right side out and insert the pillow form through the zipper opening.

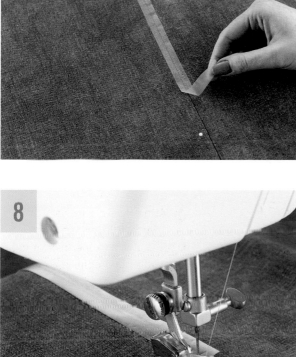

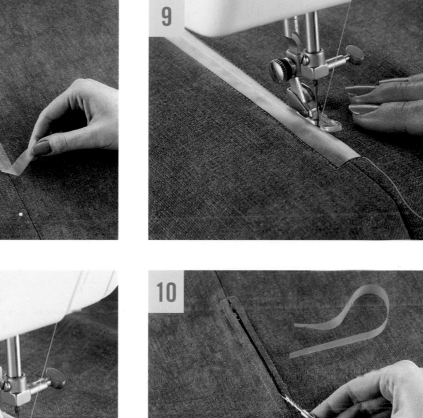

PLACEMATS and NAPKINS

Spark up your dining room table or breakfast nook with reversible octagonal placemats. These placemats are **LINED TO THE EDGE** and can be made reversible by selecting two decorator fabrics. Welting (page 7), sewn into the outer edge of the placemat, is available in different sizes and colors. For ease of application, choose welting no larger than 3/16" (4.5 mm). Make napkins to match, simply by cutting, pressing, and hemming If you want to be able to launder the placemats and napkins, choose fabrics that are washable and be sure to **PRESHRINK** the fabrics and the welting before you start cutting.

WHAT YOU'LL LEARN

How to cut fabric using a paper pattern

How to insert narrow welting into a seam

How to make neat corners and points

How to stitch a mitered double-fold hem

WHAT YOU'LL NEED

For four sets:

Craft paper for drawing a pattern

3/4 yd. (0.7 m) fabric for placemat fronts

3/4 yd. (0.7 m) fabric for placemat backs

7 yd. (6.4 m) welting

1 yd. (0.92 m) fabric for napkins

Thread to match fabrics

How to Sew a PLACEMAT

1 Draw a 13" × 19" (33 × 48.5 cm) rectangle on craft paper. Mark a point 3½" (9 cm) from each corner. Draw diagonal lines across each corner connecting marks; cut off the corners.

2 PRESHRINK the fabrics. To preshrink the welting, wrap it into large loops and tie it in the middle with a large loose knot. Soak the welting in warm water; squeeze out excess moisture. Place it in a net laundry bag or nylon stocking before tossing it in the dryer. This will keep it from getting too tangled.

3 Fold the fabric for the placemat front in half lengthwise, aligning the SELVAGES. Place the paper pattern with one short edge running parallel to and just beyond the selvages. This will ensure that the placemat is cut on-grain. Pin the pattern in place through both layers of fabric inserting pins about every 3" (7.5 cm) around the outer edge. Cut out the placemat. Remove the pins and cut two more fronts, following the same procedure. Then cut four placemat backs from the other fabric.

4 PRESS the flat edge of the welting if necessary. Pin the welting to the right side of the placemat front along the outer edge, keeping the raw edges aligned and the welting relaxed. Plan for the ends to overlap along one long edge and leave tails unpinned. *Insert the pins perpendicular to the edges (p. 19).*

TIP **Keep the welting relaxed as you pin and actually "crowd" the welting slightly at the corners so that it will lie flat when it is turned to its final position.**

5 Clip into the seam allowance of the welting at each corner of the placemat at the exact point where the welting must bend. *Clip to, but not through* the stitching line, so that the welting seam allowances spread open and lie flat. Pin securely, keeping the raw edges of the welting and placemat aligned.

6 Set the machine for a straight stitch of 10 stitches per inch, which equals 2.5 mm. Attach the zipper foot and adjust it to the right of the needle. If your foot is not adjustable, adjust the needle to the left of the foot. Place the fabric under the presser foot 2" (5 cm) from the end of the welting. Slowly stitch the welting to the fabric, stitching over the existing stitches in the welting. *Remove pins as you come to them (p. 19).*

CONTINUED

QUICK REFERENCE

Clip to, but not through. This will allow the fabric to lay smoothly without puckering when the topper is turned right side out. Be careful not to cut the stitches, or a hole will develop in the seam.

How to Sew a **PLACEMAT**

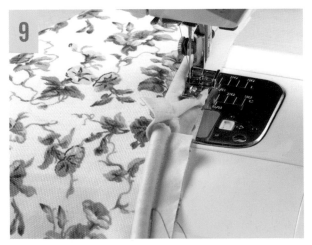

CONTINUED

7 When you reach a corner, stop with the needle down in the fabric at the point of the clip. Lift the presser foot and **PIVOT** the fabric so the stitching line of the welting on the next side is in line with the needle. Lower the presser foot and continue stitching around the placemat, pivoting at each corner.

8 Stop stitching 2" (5 cm) from the point where the ends of the welting will meet. Cut off the end of the welting so it overlaps the beginning end by 1" (2.5 cm). Remove the stitching from the overlapping end of the welting, exposing the inner cording; trim the end of the cording so it just meets the other end.

9 Fold under ½" (1.3 cm) of the fabric on the overlapping end of the welting. Wrap it around the beginning and finish stitching it to the placemat, overlapping the stitches ½" (1.3 cm) where they meet.

10 Press along the stitching line with the tip of your iron to relax the fabric and set the seam. Check that the fabric does not ripple or draw up where you have attached the welting.

11 Pin the placemat front over the back, right sides together, encasing the welting between the layers and aligning the outer edges. Leave a 7" (18 cm) opening unpinned along one side. Place the placemat under the presser foot, back side down, just ahead of the unpinned area. Remove the pin marking the end of the opening before lowering the presser foot.

12 *Backstitch (p. 19)* three or four stitches; then stitch forward *over the previous stitches,* actually "crowding" the welting with the zipper foot as you stitch. Pivot at each corner, and stop stitching at the opposite side of the opening. Backstitch three or four stitches, and *remove the fabric from the machine (p. 19).*

CONTINUED

QUICK REFERENCE

Over the previous stitches. The second stitching line must be exactly over the first stitching line or slightly closer to the welting, so that the first stitching line does not show after the placemat is turned right side out.

How to Sew a PLACEMAT

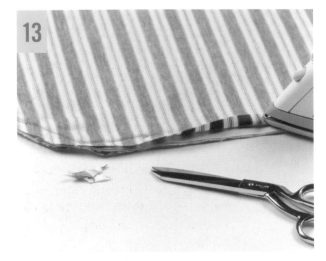

CONTINUED

---

13 *Trim the seam allowances diagonally* at each corner. Turn back and press the back seam allowance ½" (1.3 cm) from the edge in the unstitched area.

14 Reach in through the unstitched opening to grasp the opposite side of the placemat and pull it through the opening. Turn the placemat right side out.

15 Use a point turner to push out the corners, if necessary. Press the placemat up to the welting as you smooth and tug the welting out to the edge with your fingers. Slipstitch the opening closed, following the directions on page 24.

💡

QUICK REFERENCE

Trim the seam allowances diagonally. This step eliminates the excess bulk at the corners, allowing them to lie flat and square after turning the valance right side out.

How to Sew NAPKINS

1 Cut squares for the napkins 1" (2.5 cm) larger than the desired finished size. Press under ½" (1.3 cm) on each side of the napkin. Unfold the corner, and refold it diagonally so that the pressed folds match. Press the diagonal fold, and trim the corner as shown. Repeat for each corner.

TIP For the most efficient use of your fabric, cut three 15" (38 cm) squares from 45" (115 cm) fabric or 18" (46 cm) squares from 54" (137 cm) fabric.

2 Fold the raw edges under to meet the pressed fold, forming a ¼" (6 mm) *double-fold hem*. The corners will form neat diagonal folds. Press the folds; pin only if necessary.

3 Stitch the hem close to the inner fold, using a short straight stitch and beginning along one side. At the corners, stop with the needle down in the fabric, between the diagonal folds, and pivot. Overlap the stitches about ½" (1.3 cm) where they meet.

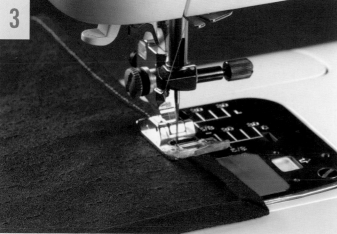

QUICK REFERENCE

Double-fold hem. Double-fold hems are made with two folds of equal depths, encasing the cut edge in the crease of the outer fold. Pressing the first fold to the total hem depth, in this case 1" (2.5 cm), allows you to be more accurate in turning and pressing.

Rod-pocket CURTAINS

Many window curtains are hung from a pole or rod by means of a "pocket" sewn along the upper edge. Thus the name, "rod-pocket" treatments. Styles vary depending on the rod or pole used, the depth of the **HEADING**, the length of the curtain or top treatment, the **FULLNESS** of the style, and the way the style is arranged once it has been mounted over the window. There are also added embellishments, such as decorative trims or tie-backs, that can give the treatment a distinctive look.

WHAT YOU'LL LEARN

How to sew a rod pocket and heading

How to use *drapery weights*

WHAT YOU'LL NEED

Fabric, amount determined by working through the chart on page 48

Thread to match fabric

Curtain rod or pole

Drapery weights if sewing curtains

For now, though, let's just focus on a basic rod-pocket valance and identify its parts. The diagram below shows that the valance is really a flat rectangle of fabric. The sides and bottom of the rectangle are hemmed with *double-fold hems (p. 45).* The top is folded to the back and sewn with two stitching lines. The heading, from the top fold to the top stitching line, forms a ruffle above the rod when the valance is mounted. The area between the stitching lines is the **ROD POCKET**. Designed to have two times fullness, the rectangle is made twice as wide as the desired **FINISHED WIDTH** of the valance. Note that this valance requires two widths of fabric. One is centered and the other is cut in half and sewn to each side, thus avoiding a distracting center seam.

HEADING

ROD POCKET

SIDE HEM · SEAM · SEAM · SIDE HEM

BOTTOM HEM

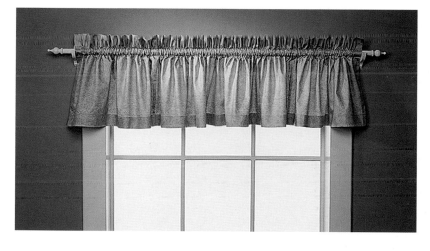

To determine the rod-pocket depth (**A**), measure around the widest part of the rod or pole. In some cases this may mean measuring in the crook of an elbow. Add ½" (1.3 cm) **EASE** to this measurement, and divide the result by 2. This measurement will be the distance between stitching lines.

The height of the heading (**B**) can be adjusted to suit your taste, from very short at ½" (1.3 cm) to quite high at 4" (10 cm). Sometimes the heading is made extremely long so that it falls forward over the rod pocket, forming an attached valance along the top of a rod-pocket curtain.

QUICK REFERENCE

Drapery weights. Drapery weights make your curtains hang better at the sides by pulling gently and constantly on the side hems. Inserted between the layers of the bottom hem, they are "trapped" in place when you stitch the side hem. Because they are made of metal, avoid hitting them with the needle.

How to Sew a ROD-POCKET CURTAIN

1

Finished length, measured from the bottom of the rod to the bottom of the treatment:	12" (30.5 cm)
Add the total hem depth	+ 4" (10 cm)
Add the rod pocket depth twice	+ 1¾" (4.5 cm)
	+ 1¾" (4.5 cm)
Add the heading height twice	+ 2½" (6.5 cm)
	+ 2½" (6.5 cm)
Add ½" (1.3 cm) to turn under bottom of rod pocket	+ ½" (1.3 cm)
Add ½" (1.3 cm) for ease	+ ½" (1.3 cm)
to find the CUT LENGTH of each piece*	= 25½" (64.8 cm)
Multiply the window width	36" (91.5 cm)
by the desired fullness	× 2½
to find the finished width	= 90" (229 cm)
Add the total side hem depth twice	+ 2" (5 cm)
	+ 2" (5 cm)
To find the total CUT WIDTH needed	= 94" (239 cm)
Divide the total cut width by the fabric width	÷ 54" (137 cm)
Round the number up to the nearest whole number	= 1.74
to find the number of fabric widths needed	2
Multiply this number by the cut length	× 25½" (64.8 cm)
to find the length to buy	= 51" (129.5 cm)

Because fabric stores sell fabric in whole yards (meters) or eighths of a yard (fractions of a meter), purchase the next largest amount. If you buy a fabric with a **PATTERN REPEAT**, follow the chart until you have determined the cut length*. Your actual cut length must be rounded up to the next number evenly divisible by the pattern repeat. For instance, if the pattern repeat is 15" (38 cm), your cut length will be 30" (76 cm), not 25½" (64.8 cm), because 30 (76) can be evenly divided by 15 (38). Proceed with the chart using this revised cut length measurement.

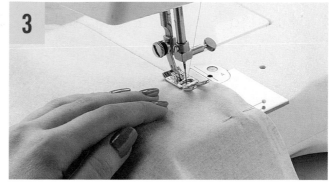

LET'S BEGIN

1 Measure the window and calculate the length of fabric needed for your valance or curtain, working with the formula, opposite: (We used these numbers for our valance on page 46, your numbers will probably be different.)

2 **PRESHRINK** your fabric. Measure and mark the location of each cut along the **SELVAGE**. Cut the pieces, following the cutting guidelines on page 10. If you do not have to match a pattern, cut away the selvages, cutting just beyond the tightly woven area.

3 Pin two pieces together along the vertical edges, *inserting the pins perpendicular to the edges (p. 19).* Match the pattern, if necessary. Stitch ½" (1.3 cm) **SEAM**, *backstitching (p. 19)* at the beginning and end of the seam for about ½" (1.3 cm). *Remove pins as you come to them (p. 19).*

QUICK REFERENCE

Finished length. Valances are not only decorative, they also "cap" the window visually and hide mechanical workings of any undertreatments. As a general proportion guideline, the valance length is about one-fifth of the total distance from the top of the window to the floor. You can make your valance longer or shorter, if you prefer. Sketch the total window treatment to scale to help you make this decision.

Measure from the bottom of the rod. If you have not yet installed the rod, or even selected a rod, plan to install it so that the bottom of the rod is even with the top of the window frame. Then you can measure from the top of the frame to where you want the bottom edge of the valance or curtain to be.

Round up to the nearest whole number. Most window treatments that have some amount of fullness in them, including rod-pocket treatments, are sewn using full and half widths of fabric. Even if your treatment requires two-and-one-half widths of fabric, you have to purchase three full widths, and your yardage requirements have to be determined by rounding up to the nearest whole number.

CONTINUED

How to Sew a ROD-POCKET CURTAIN

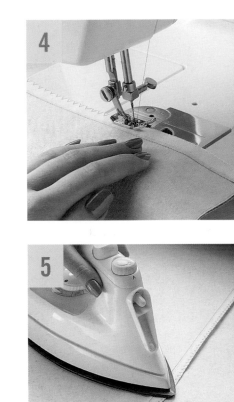

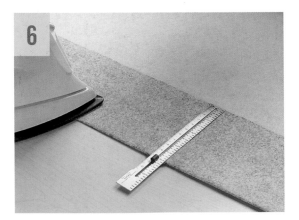

4 Finish the raw edges together, using a zigzag stitch (page 21) set at medium width and medium length. Stitch so the right-hand swing of the needle just clears the fabric edge.

5 Repeat steps 3 and 4 until you have sewn all the pieces together across the valance or curtain width. If there are any *half widths,* sew them onto an end. **PRESS** all of the seam allowances to one side.

6 Place the valance or curtain facedown on an ironing surface. Press under the lower edge 4" (10 cm) for the hem.

7 Unfold the pressed edge. Turn the cut edge back, aligning it to the pressed foldline; press the outer fold.

8 Refold the hem along the pressed foldlines, encasing the raw edge to form a 2" (5 cm) *double-fold hem (p. 45).* Pin the hem, inserting the pins perpendicular to the foldlines.

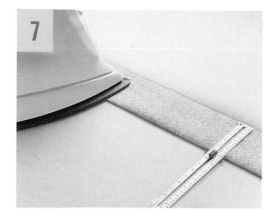

QUICK REFERENCE

Half widths are always added at the outer edge of a valance or curtain panel. The seam is sewn along the edge that had the selvage; the side hem is sewn along the edge that was the center of the fabric width. (This is the only way you are able to match the pattern, if there is one.) Also, half panels go on the side of the treatment nearest the **RETURN.**

9 Place the hem under the presser foot of the machine, with the wrong side of the valance or curtain facing up. The bulk of the fabric is positioned to the left of the machine. The side edge should be even with the back of the presser foot, with the needle aligned to enter the fabric just inside the inner fold.

10 Stitch the hem along the inner fold, backstitching at the beginning and end about ½" (1.3 cm). Remove pins as you come to them.

TIP Double-fold side hems measure a total of 2" (5 cm): 1" (2.5 cm) turned under twice. Double-fold bottom hems on valances measure a total of 4" (10 cm): 2" (5 cm) turned under twice. Double-fold bottom hems on curtains measure a total of 8" (20.5 cm): 4" (10 cm) turned under twice.

CONTINUED

CONTINUED

---

11 Repeat steps 6 to 10 for the side hems, pressing under 2" (5 cm) first, instead of 4" (10 cm).

12 Press under ½" (1.3 cm) along the upper edge. Then, measuring from the pressed foldline, press under an amount equal to the heading height plus the rod-pocket depth. (Check your measurement from step 1.) Insert pins along the lower foldline.

13 Place the folded upper edge under the presser foot of the machine, with the wrong side of the valance or curtain facing up. The bulk of the fabric is positioned to the left of the machine. The side hem should be even with the back of the presser foot, with the needle aligned to enter the fabric along the lower fold.

14 Stitch along the lower fold, across the entire width; backstitch about ½" (1.3 cm) at the beginning and the end. Remove pins as you come to them. This stitching line is the bottom of the rod pocket.

15 Measure the heading height, measuring on the wrong side, from the upper fold. Mark the stitching line, using chalk or an erasable marking pen. Pin frequently through both layers along the stitching line, inserting pins perpendicular to the line.

16 Stitch along the marked line across the entire width; backstitch at the beginning and end of the line. Remove pins as you come to them. This stitching line is the top of the rod pocket.

17 Press the valance or curtain one more time. Insert the rod into the rod pocket. Mount the rod on the brackets, following the instructions that came with the rod. Distribute the fullness evenly along the rod.

TIP Tape a small plastic bag over the end of the rod to make it slide more easily into the rod pocket.

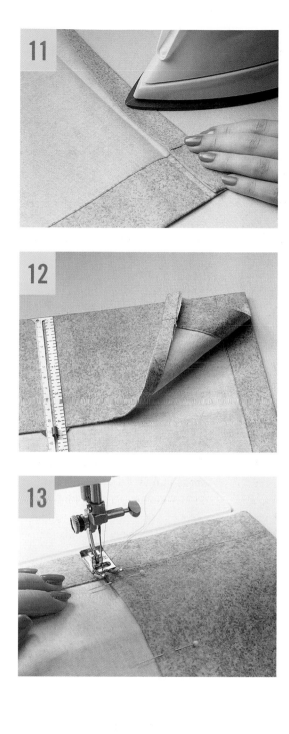

Simple SKIRTS

Skirts with elastic waistbands are classic, comfortable, and easy-care. Straight or flared versions in varying lengths can be coordinated with a variety of sweaters or other tops for business, dress, or casual wear. Check the pattern envelope for recommended fabrics. Some patterns are designed only for knits and generally fit the body closer, counting on the stretchiness of the fabric to allow you to slide the skirt over your hips. Patterns suitable for woven fabrics will include extra fullness. The first set of directions works for woven or knit fabrics. Alternate steps for sewing with knits begin on page 61. These directions may differ from your pattern; be sure to use the **SEAM ALLOWANCE** given in your pattern. Select a pattern with two pieces: a front and a back. An elastic **CASING** at the waistline is formed from excess fabric length at the skirt top. The skirt itself may be constructed of two, three, or four sections, depending on whether or not there are center front or back **SEAMS**.

WHAT YOU'LL LEARN

How to adjust a pattern

Two methods for sewing elastic waistlines

Hem alternatives for skirts

How to sew and finish seams

WHAT YOU'LL NEED

Skirt pattern with elastic waistline

Fabric (check pattern for amount)

Matching all-purpose thread

1" (2.5 cm) nonroll elastic, enough to go around your waist

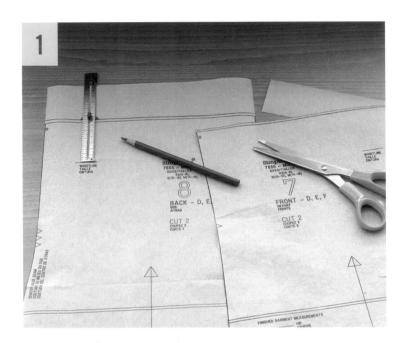

LET'S BEGIN

1 To construct the skirt following these directions, 2¾" (7 cm) of fabric must be allowed for the casing above the waistline. This may be different from the casing allowance already on your pattern. Measure this distance from the waistline, and mark a cutting line on your pattern. (Add extra paper, if necessary.) Be sure to mark both front and back pattern pieces.

2 **PRESHRINK** and **PRESS** the fabric, lay out the pattern (page 12), and cut the fabric (page 16). Transfer any necessary marks (page 17). Insert a size 11/70 or 12/80 sharp or universal sewing machine needle. If your pattern does not have center front or back seams, move on to step 4. If your pattern has a center front seam, place the skirt front pieces right sides together, aligning the center cut edges and matching the notches. *Insert pins perpendicular to the sides (p. 19).*

TIP Be sure you are not pinning the pieces together along the side seams. Sometimes it is difficult to tell the difference. Check your pattern to be sure.

3 Place the fabric under the presser foot with the cut edges aligned to the ⅝" (1.5 cm) seam allowance guide. Stitch the center front seam, *backstitching (p. 19)* a few stitches at the upper and lower edges, and *removing pins as you come to them (p.19)*. If your pattern has a center back seam, stitch it in the same manner.

TIP If your skirt has side seam pockets, follow the pattern directions carefully, as methods vary.

4 If it is difficult to tell the skirt front from the skirt back, mark the wrong side of the skirt back, using chalk. Place the front and back skirt pieces right sides together, aligning the side edges and matching the notches. Insert pins perpendicular to the center front seam. Stitch the side seams, backstitching at the upper and lower edges, and removing pins as you come to them. If you are sewing on a woven fabric, finish (page 21) the edges of all the seam allowances.

5 PRESS all the seams flat to set the stitching line in the fabric. This may seem unnecessary, but it really does give you a better-looking seam in the end. Then press the seam allowances open.

TIP To prevent the cut edge of the seam allowance from imprinting the front of the fabric, press seams open over a seam roll or hard cardboard tube.

CONTINUED

CONTINUED

---

6 BASTE the seam allowances open flat from the upper edge down about 4" (10 cm) (arrows). This will keep them from getting in the way when you insert the elastic in step 9. Finish the waistline edge, using a multistitch-zigzag (page 21). Fold the upper edge 1½" (3.8 cm) to the wrong side, and press. Insert pins along and perpendicular to the fold.

7 EDGESTITCH close to the fold around the upper edge of the waistline. Begin and end at a side seam, overlapping the stitches about ½" (1.3 cm).

TIP Sometimes it is difficult to tell the skirt front from the back when the garment is finished. We've sewn a short loop of twill tape under the casing seam to identify the back.

8 Insert pins along the lower edge of the casing. Place a piece of tape on the bed of your machine 1¼" (3.2 cm) from the tip of the needle. Stitch the lower edge of the casing, guiding the upper edge along the tape. Leave a 2" (5 cm) opening at one side seam.

9 Fasten a safety pin or bodkin (page 7) to one end of the elastic, and insert the elastic through the casing opening. Push and pull the safety pin all the way to the opposite side of the opening. Remove the basting threads from step 6.

TIP Insert a large safety pin across the free end of the elastic so that it will not get pulled into the opening.

10 Try on the skirt. Pull up the elastic to fit your waist snugly, yet comfortably; pin the ends together.

11 Take off the skirt. Pull the pinned ends of the elastic several inches (centimeters) out of the casing. Trim the overlapped ends to ½" (1.3 cm), if necessary. Place them under the presser foot, and stitch through both layers, using a multistitch-zigzag.

CONTINUED

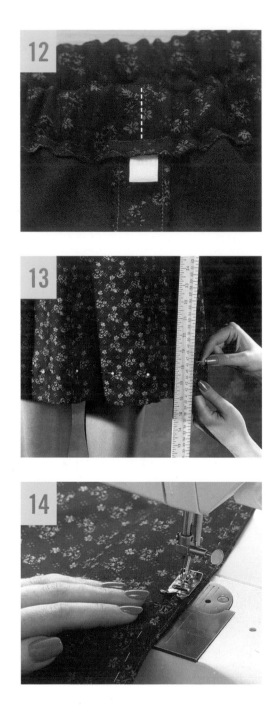

CONTINUED

12 Machine-stitch the opening in the casing closed. Distribute the casing fullness evenly around the elastic. *Stitch in the ditch* at the seams to keep the elastic from shifting or rolling.

13 Try on the skirt, and have someone *mark the hem length* for you, using chalk or pins.

14 Take off the skirt, and trim the hem allowance to an even depth. (Check the pattern for hem allowance.) Turn under the hem along the markings, and pin. For double-fold hems on slightly flared skirts, it is helpful to hand-baste on the inner fold. Stitch the hem by hand (page 22) or by machine (page 23); select a method that will allow the hem to stretch, if you are using a knit. Give the skirt a final pressing, and give yourself a pat on the back.

1 To construct a knit skirt following these directions, an amount of fabric equal to *twice the width of the elastic* must be allowed above the waistline. Measure this distance from the waistline, and mark a new cutting line on your pattern. (Add extra paper, if necessary.) Be sure to mark both front and back pattern pieces. Follow steps 2 to 5 on pages 56 and 57, sewing with the seam allowances designated by your pattern. It is not necessary to finish seams on knit skirts.

TIP Read your pattern directions. Some patterns, especially those that have ¼" (6 mm) seam allowances, instruct you to sew your elastic waistline with this method. There is no need to alter those patterns, as they already allow this amount of fabric at the top.

2 Cut a piece of elastic to fit your waist snugly, yet still stretch to fit over your hips. Overlap the ends ½" (1.3 cm), and stitch them together, using a wide zigzag stitch or multistitch-zigzag. Divide both the elastic and the upper edge of the skirt into fourths, and pin-mark. Pin the elastic to the wrong side of the skirt, aligning the edges and matching the pin marks; insert the pins perpendicular to the edges.

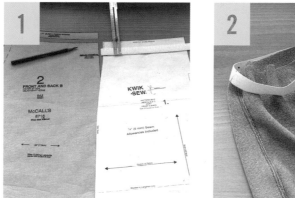

QUICK REFERENCE

Stitch in the ditch. Stitching from the right side and using short stitches, stitch directly into the well of the seam. Your stitches will practically disappear.

Mark the hem length. During the marking, stand straight, wearing the shoes you will be wearing with the skirt. The person marking should measure up from the floor to the desired length, moving around you as necessary. Otherwise, the hem will be uneven. If you don't have help, turn up the hem to the desired length and check in a mirror for even length.

Twice the width of the elastic. For this method, 1" (2.5 cm) elastic works well, though you may decide to use a different width. Some specialty elastics have channels for topstitching, giving the look of multiple rows.

CONTINUED

CONTINUED

3 Insert four more pins, evenly spaced, between the quarter marks, distributing the fabric fullness evenly. Set your machine for a medium-width multistitch-zigzag. Place the skirt under the presser foot with the elastic on top. Align the edge of the foot to the elastic and fabric edges. Stitch, *stretching the elastic to fit between the pins* and keeping the edges aligned. Remove pins as you come to them, stopping with the needle down in the fabric.

4 Fold the elastic to the wrong side of the skirt, so the fabric encases the elastic. From the right side of the skirt, *stitch in the ditch (p. 61)* of the seam through all the waistband layers, at each seam. This step makes step 5 easier.

TIP Stretch the waistband slightly to give yourself a clear view of your target.

5 With the right side facing up, **TOPSTITCH** through all layers of the waistband, stretching the elastic as you sew. Use either a zigzag or multistitch-zigzag, with medium width and length, and stitch near the lower edge of the elastic. These stitches will allow the skirt to stretch as it goes over your hips. Finish the skirt, following steps 13 and 14 on page 60.

QUICK REFERENCE

Stretching the elastic to fit between the pins.
Grasp the fabric and elastic behind the presser foot with one hand and ahead of the presser foot with the other hand, working in small sections at a time. Stretch the elastic only far enough to take up the slack in the fabric. Keep an even tension on the elastic, allowing the feed dogs to feed the fabric at a steady pace. Stop sewing to move your hands.

GLOSSARY

APPLIQUÉ. This French word refers to a decoration or cutout that is applied to the surface of a larger piece of fabric. Many methods of appliqué are used, including simply machine stitching around the outline of the decoration.

BASTE. Long, easy-to-remove, straight stitches are sewn into the fabric temporarily, either by hand or by machine.

BIAS refers to the diagonal direction of a piece of fabric. True bias is at a 45-degree angle to both the lengthwise and crosswise grains. Woven fabric has considerable stretch on the bias.

CASING. A fabric tunnel, through which something will be inserted, is sewn into an item. One example is the rod pocket at the top of a curtain panel. A casing can also hold a drawstring or elastic.

COURSES. Corresponding to the crosswise grain of a woven fabric, the courses of a knit fabric run perpendicular to the selvages and ribs. Knit fabrics are most stretchy in the direction of the courses.

CROSSWISE GRAIN. On woven fabric, the crosswise grain runs perpendicular to the selvages. Fabric has slight "give" on the crosswise grain.

CUT LENGTH refers to the total length at which fabric should be cut for a project. It includes allowances for hems, seams, rod pockets and matching prints.

CUT WIDTH refers to the total width at which fabric should be cut for a project. If more than one width of fabric is needed, the cut width refers to the entire panel after seams are sewn, including allowances for any side hems or seams.

EASE. Some fabric length, beyond what you have calculated, will be "eaten up" by turning under and stitching any double-fold hems, heading, or rod pocket. Also, when a treatment is gathered onto a rod, the length may "shrink up" a bit. By adding ½" (1.3 cm) to the length before cutting, your finished length will be more accurate.

EDGESTITCH. With the machine set for straight stitching at a length of 2 to 2.5 mm or 10 stitches per inch, stitch within ⅛" (3 mm) of a finished edge. With many machines, this can be achieved by guiding the inner edge of the right presser foot toe along the outer finished edge.

FINISHED WIDTH refers to the total width of a project after it is sewn. For a tablecloth, this includes the table width plus twice the drop length. For an inside-mounted Roman shade, the finished width is the inside width of the window frame; for an outside-mounted shade, the finished width includes the window frame width plus 1" (2.5 cm) beyond the frame on both sides.

FULLNESS describes the finished width of a curtain in proportion to the length of the rod. For example, two times fullness means that the width of the curtain measures two times the length of the rod.

GRAINLINES. Woven fabrics have two grainlines, lengthwise and crosswise, which coincide with the yarns running in both directions at right angles to each other. In order for a finished project to hang or lay straight, horizontal and vertical cuts must follow the grainlines exactly.

HEADING is the portion at the top of a rod-pocket window treatment that forms a ruffle when the curtain is on the rod. The depth of the heading is the distance from the finished upper edge to the top stitching line for the rod pocket.

LENGTHWISE GRAIN. On woven fabric, the lengthwise grain runs parallel to the selvages. Fabrics are generally stronger along the lengthwise grain.

LINED TO THE EDGE means that a fabric panel is backed with lining that is cut to the exact same size. The two pieces are joined together by a seam around the outer edge, with the raw edges of the seam allowances concealed between the layers.

NAP. Some fabrics have definite "up" and "down" directions, either because of a surface pile, like corduroy or velveteen, or because of a one-way print. When laying out a pattern on napped fabric, cut all the pieces with the top edges facing the same direction.

PATTERN REPEAT, a characteristic of decorator fabrics, is the lengthwise distance from one distinctive point in the pattern, such as the tip of a petal in a floral motif, to the exact same point in the next motif.

CONTINUED

GLOSSARY

CONTINUED

PIVOT. Perfect corners are stitched by stopping with the needle down in the fabric at the exact corner before turning the fabric. To be sure the corner stitch locks, tburn the handwheel until the needle goes all the way down and just begins to rise.

PRESHRINK. Fabric that shrinks, especially natural fibers, shrinks most in the first laundering. If you intend to launder your finished item occasionally, you should wash the fabric before cutting out the pieces, so the item will not shrink after you make it. "Dry clean only" fabrics can be preshrunk by steaming them with your iron.

PRESSING. This step is extremely important to the success of your sewing projects. Select the heat setting appropriate for your fabric and use steam. Lift and lower the iron in an overlapping pattern. Do not slide the iron down the seam, as this can cause the fabric to stretch out of shape, especially on the crosswise grain or bias.

RETURN is the portion of the curtain or top treatment extending from the end of the rod or mounting board to the wall, blocking the side light and view.

RIBS. Corresponding to the lengthwise grain in woven fabric, the ribs of a knit fabric run parallel to the selvages (if there are any). Knits are usually most stable in the rib direction.

ROD POCKET is a stitched fabric tunnel in a curtain where the curtain rod or pole is inserted. Stitching lines at the top and bottom of the pocket keep the rod or pole in place.

ROTARY CUTTER AND MAT. These time-saving tools for cutting fabric may also take a little practice and serious precautions. The blade on a rotary cutter is extremely sharp. Cut slowly, watch your fingers, and always retract or cover the blade between cuts. The rotary cutter cannot be used without the special protective mat.

SEAM. Two pieces of fabric are placed right sides together and joined near the edge with stitches. After stitching, the raw edges are hidden on the wrong side, leaving a clean, smooth line on the right side.

SEAM ALLOWANCE. Narrow excess fabric between the stitching line and the raw edge gives the seam strength and ensures that the stitches cannot be pulled off the raw edges.

SELVAGES. Characteristic of woven fabrics, these narrow, tightly woven outer edges should be cut away, or they may cause seams to pucker and may shrink excessively when laundered.

TEMPORARY FABRIC ADHESIVE. Available in a convenient spray can, this product can be used to hold two fabric pieces together temporarily until they are stitched together permanently. The adhesive is light and colorless, and will not gum up the sewing machine needle. Some brands of the adhesive simply diminish after a few weeks. Others can be removed by laundering.

THREAD JAM. No matter how conscientious you are, threads can become tangled up in a wad under the fabric and cause the machine to get "stuck." DON'T USE FORCE! Remove the presser foot, if you can. Snip all the threads you can reach from the top of the throat plate. Open the bobbin case door or throat plate, and snip away threads until you can remove the bobbin. Gently remove the fabric. Thoroughly clean out the feed dog and bobbin area before reinserting the bobbin and starting over. Then just chalk it up to experience and get over it!

TOPSTITCHING is a decorative and functional stitching line placed ¼" to 1" (6 mm to 2.5 cm) from the finished edge of an item. The stitching is done with the right side of the item facing up. Sometimes topstitching is done with a heavier thread or two threads through the machine needle, to make it more visible.

ZIGZAG STITCH. In this setting, the needle alternately moves from left to right with each stitch. You can alter the width of the needle swing as well as the length between stitches. A zigzag stitch that is twice as wide as it is long gives you a balanced stitch, appropriate for finishing seam allowances.